JUST ANOTHER FRIDAY NIGHT IN BROOKLYN

JIM HART

Hart, Jim
ISBN: 9798742829492
Just Another Friday Night in Brooklyn/Jim Hart – 1st ed.

Printed in the USA

JUST ANOTHER FRIDAY NIGHT IN BROOKLYN

BOOKS BY JIM HART

POETRY

RAMBLINGS OF A ONE-EYED GARBAGE MAN
A HANDFUL OF SMOKE
JUST ANOTHER FRIDAY NIGHT IN BROOKLYN

NOVELS

(The Harry Parker Mystery Series)
A TOM COLLINS TO GO
THE AVIATION COCKTAIL

For The Guys Of My Brooklyn Youth
Who Never Got To Grow Old

CONTENTS

REMEMBERING

In the August hot Brooklyn night
I wake
reminded of death's universal sadness

Eddie and Carmel
fallen to their ends
from the same Sixty-Fifth Street building
one day minus one year apart

Each
found by Skinny
taking the back-alley shortcut
to our Sixty-Forth Street hangout

Sitting up in bed
realizing Skinny too is gone
too much juice in the needle

And Head who provided Skinny with the shot
and dumped him – cold – on the movie theater steps
later killed in a deal gone wrong

My cold sweat
drying
as I realize how lucky I was
to have found music and poetry
and written myself
a different ending

JUST ANOTHER FRIDAY NIGHT IN BROOKLYN

The brown bottle
with the whisky label
was harder to break
than he thought

Three times
against the bar's edge
before it became
the shard edge weapon he desired

The two
were quick upon him
their threats
turned to deeds that fast

Only one
caught his face slashing anger
before the other's stool
caught him

The glass candle flames
sputtered
and shadows
leapt above his head

But even drunk
he kept his quick movements
rolling like the man on fire
he was

And up he stood
jagged bottle
still
in hand

And payback
like they say
is
a bitch

And only he
was left
to pay
the bill

But money
like
a reputation
can be earned

So
he smiled
peeling off
the Benjamin's

And victory
is much
much
sweeter

When realizing
that history
is written
by the victor

LOST

The shrill screams
vanishing
in the crackling flames
just beyond
the fireman's crying eyes

JAZZED

It's midnight
in the junkie needle back alley
And his glazed-eyes
are filled with the nothingness
of pain so dulled
he doesn't even feel the broken glass
cutting into his can't get up ass
He is off on a voyage
of vein rush devotion
Shaky hands waving shaky matches
trying to light shaky lip held joint
And somewhere – way back in his head
Coltrane's "Body and Soul" is riffing
And his long dead mother's voice
tries to break through with "baby you're late for school"
which seems like a bygone warning
about jaundice or AIDS or playing ball in the street
or something else – he just can't lay his finger on
And his mouth is now so dry
it tastes like an old dirty sock
and he takes a second to laugh – out loud
wondering how he knows what an old dirty sock tastes like
And then he's off
I mean seeing it all
stretched out before him
as clear and straight as a two-lane highway
from New Mexico to Nevada
Knowing for sure
that this ride doesn't need refueling
and no sirens or red flashing lights
are gonna stop it
till he reaches – the end of the road

STILL NOT WANTING TO FALL ASLEEP

In our sleep
we can go home
and phantasmagorically Mom and Dad are still alive
as are All the brothers

And the big black dog roams the backyard
guarding the house from invasion by each passing N train

Stickball games are being played in the street
accompanied by the loud horn blare of a 1957 American
well made
two tons of steel light green Pontiac
driven by the old Jewish couple
who live in the apartment building across the street
and work in the laundromat they own
Saying "Don do it - Don do it" in thick Brooklyn Jewish
accents
to all the ballplayers who run and throw the ball
while they are getting in or out of their car

The game halted only - for us - the Hart Boys
by Dad's better-be-here-now for dinner whistle
that penetrated the distance from our stoop to wherever we
were
with fear frightened audible awareness beyond canine
capabilities

Aware - in passing - of his job well done smile
as we rush past him up the stairs to wash our hands
fighting for the soap the sink and the towel in that order
to get back down and be seated at the table
that Mom had set each and every night

And that she'd clear after we ate
so we could begin that arduous journey through, Math-
English-Geography -Religion-
Catholic school homework
ending the night just late enough for no TV time before
bed

Not wanting to fall asleep
knowing you had to get up and start the school day all over
again
which now seemed like the perfect preparation for life

And then you wake
alone
to the cold sweat realization
that all is not well in the world

That Annette - your seven-year-old crush-is no longer a
Mouseketeer

That Mom and Dad are gone
and brothers Joe and John
And the big black dog watched his last N train three
decades ago

And you are older than your father in those happy years
you thought so bad

And your children are now almost his age then

And the strange realization that you and your brother are
the last of your generation
the old men of your uncles and family friends age

And are certainly
next in line
to go

FORGETTING NOT TO LOOK

Inherited as language and pain
the born addicted baby
cries out in the dark of day

Blind and craving
for juices not of the breast

The nurse stands heart heavy
dumbfounded - motionless
as if she'd been fit by some mob guys
for cement shoes and overcoat

Only her head moving
in tear-filled
tremoring noes

Each time witnessing
as if the first

GLASSES ON HIS PILLOW

He walks in photographer's badly lit shadows
a lying smile slicing across his face

Forty-seven years old
never married

Who would have guessed
The same bartender serves him some slop
from the one-page greasy menu
every night
and refills his glass five times
as whatever season's ballgame
winds down on the high shelf-low-volume color fading
analog TV

The newspaper
left behind by a co-worker
or fellow train rider
he saves for his one room bed

Tonight fixated
on the story of some poor lonely guy
threw himself out his fourth floor walkup window

I AM THE MURDERER OF 41st STREET

Noises
heard from
third floor window
Crowd
gathered
around something un-seeable
I go down to investigate

A dog has been run over by a car
cut him in half
Literally
two pieces
one beside the other

Yelping sounds
still somehow coming from his undead
shaking
mouth
I lean over
pet his head
and choke him
to silence

The women scream
turning the heads of their children
The men pull back
from the shame
of their lack of courage

"All the king's horses . . ."
I feel like shouting
but know it would do no good

Later in the afternoon
the garbage truck came
and unceremoniously delivered him to his incinerated end

For months
my "neighbors"
pointed in whispers
crossing the street

Careful not to meet up
with
Jim the Ripper

HITTING A WALL AT SIXTY YEARS PER MINUTE

I used to be more
Upright
Shoulders not so round
Knees not so buckled
Legs not so bowed or spindly
Voice not so quivering
in weakness of conviction
Stomach well set in
under chest
I had hair
and every tooth my own
I did not need quarterly doctor checkups
like a '57 Chevy with a mechanic's constant tinkering

Young
beautiful women
did not smile
that
Hello – helpless old man
pitying
why not
he couldn't hit on me anyway
sardonic smirk

I used to be more
Much
Much
more

REALITY CHECK

"What's the price on this, Cal?"
She said holding the box at a height you'd never think
she could achieve given her vertically challenged proportion

Yet still managing to display – perfectly – the unmistakable
Trojan helmet on the box of suddenly everybody else in the store
staring at - condoms.

"Buzz, Buzz, Buzz," Cal's disembodied voice seemed to reply
over the too heavy on the
bass storewide speaker system.

"Thank you." She whispered at a disciple level only rank amateur
seismologists mistook
for a 4.3 on the Richter scale.

Ever so slowly lowering her first place prize winning trout from
the pictures snapped held
aloft position while beginning her Bible Study rendition of why I
shouldn't use them –

Then changing suddenly to a more Christian – almost forgiving
attitude with – "Well – I
guess in today's society – you'll never know who you'll . . .
meet."

"Oh – I'm sure your daughter's a clean, practical girl." I said,
with a smile DaVinci
couldn't have chiseled off my face.

TABLE FOR ONE

"I know everything there is to know!"
She says
"Everything except this
Everything except you and her
Everything except the one thing I needed most to know"

"You didn't need to know…"
I begin but realize I'm only making it worse
realize there is no making it better
realize the strong possibility that
there is no longer an   Us

Her eyes
white hot
rivet their way through
to the tiny – still thinking
section of my brain
and I close my mouth
and turn to face the relative safety
of the blank white wall

"How Could You!"
She demands
in a volume and pitch
reached only by betrayed wives
and heard only
(if the neighbor's un-rescuing silence is interpreted
correctly)
by the men who betray them

"I…"
catch the muscle that controls speech
(I believe seventh facial)
with all the power of my will
and wrestle it to a depth of silence

unreached by the bravest submarine commander
to ever dive beneath the sea
and I have fixed my stare
on a spot on the wall
the size of a gnat's eye

And am straining for inner peace
when the sound of opening drawers
and filling suitcases
followed by the slamming door
confirms my earlier suspicion
that
We
can so quickly become
a singular form of expression

CALCULATING

His face and arms
and I don't know where else
wear those purpley blotchy birthmarks
that some people call wine marks
Though in his case
grape jelly lumpy would be more accurate

What is not purple reddens
at the closeness
no less the speech of a woman

He has lived his forty-three years
alone
Well – at least since seventeen
when his parents were killed in a car crash

He shops in the same stores
works for the same boss
all – in the neighborhood
No traveling
Easier to avoid contact

He has it all figured out
down to the precise number of pills needed
for someone of his bodyweight
for when the nights
finally become
unbearable

FEBRUARY HEAT WAVE

It was hard to imagine
harder to watch

My father
floating
in – and – out
of coherence

"Who The Hell Are You!"
"I'm Jim – your son."

A scary thing
watching the toughest man in the world
dying by degrees

GOOD MORNING – GOOD BYE

It was a good kiss
that carried through on passion
but somehow
I just knew – it wasn't a lasting – kiss

It wasn't a Main Street
middle of the day
who gives a shit who's looking
carry you into the night before you knew it – kiss

It wasn't a three years from now
sitting at an outdoor café
seeing a pretty girl saunter by
make me think of you – kiss

It wasn't a standing by the oven
old – retired – alone
whishing I'd made that other decision
and stayed more than just this night – kiss

WITH NO FORGIVENESS IN MY HEART
(1/10/75)

We went – my brother Joe and I
to the Housing Project my father worked at
and was mugged in
to collect his personal belongings
from his locker

The locker-room full of coworkers
looking at the floor – or at each other
but definitely – definitely
not at us

The door to the locker-room
had a square glass panel
that looked out onto a courtyard
and one of my father's coworkers described what
happened to him

I dropped my father's Housing Authority jacket
and jumped over a table and onto his throat
squeezing and punching for all I was worth

My brother grabbed me – and pulled me off
"What the fuck are you doing!" He demanded
"Didn't you hear him," I screamed

"He was describing what happened to Dad
which means he stood in here and watched
He Did Nothing
while Dad was being mugged
Dad!
who would have been the first to help this piece of shit."

The rest of the men did nothing
Just
as I suppose
they had done
on the most tragic day of my life

THE JAZZMEN

They play
through the dawn red hours
of night

The jazzmen
saxophones bending long cool notes
drums tap, tap, rapping
sweat soaked beat

Slippery slick
no sheet music
unfolded

The jazzmen
trumpets to their lips
eighth – sixteenth – thirty-second note riffs

Play that thing
through your pint of gin
and three hand-rolled
inspiration sticks – not so thin

The jazzmen
living between midnight and Chi town
six AM and Norleans
wiping out their axes
at every place the bus don't stop
'cause that's where the music's at

THE SOUND OF NO BRAKES STOPPING

She pushes her baby carriage
into the street
before her

Like a miner's canary
fluttering out danger

It's a black carriage
on a two a m
dimly lit street

And the baby boy
two months young
does not
keel over as gently
as the tiny
caged bird

OUTLINES

What mechanism
triggers the triggers
of debasers and murderers
of women and children

Always – it seems
self-absorbed nobodies
passing through life unnoticed

"He was quiet"
"A loner"
"Kept to himself"
Quotes from the peripheral acquaintances
of his peripheral life

No one
knew him

Authorities told us:
"He is almost always white."
"Extremely standoffish."
"Probably killed or tortured animals as a youth."
"Unnaturally close relationship with his overbearing
mother."
"Father weak – or long out of the picture."

Sometimes
but always too late for too many
these media saturated profiles
create anonymous tips
from those varied acquaintances
finally looking past the yield signs
of his innocent looking soft spoken shyness
that blended chameleon-like into their lives

And captured he exudes confidence
in his yearned for apprehension
he is talkative – open – frank
seizing his chance for attention

"It's all in slow motion
"I watch them beg – then die in slow motion." He snorts.

"You'll find them in a wooded area
along a stretch of highway
that runs east to west.
There are many more of them
than you can ever imagine."

And there it is
The statement he knew all along he'd play
the one that will take the death penalty off the table

They cannot resist giving
the "closure" answers
to so many parents
husbands – brothers – sisters

But he could not foresee
Detective Bernie O'Reilly
or how even the small favor
of an extra hour in the yard a day
for a guy pulling three consecutive life sentences
would play out
with a perfectly shoved shank
deep in his pitch-black heart

SEVENTY-THREE - AND STILL PINNING MITTENS TO COATS

They are the "gifted" children
At least that's what it says above the school door
And I watch the faces
of all the people passing as they exit
Twenty-Thirty-Forty something's
holding partners hands until their aged parents
gather them at curbside
The passing faces
wandering
wondering
what on earth could make them "gifted"

Un-imagining of the love
unconditional
they grace us with

EVERYWHERE SHE GOES

She tries
too hard
to fill the empty spaces
left by him gone

She turns herself
inside out
looking for inner places
to hang
his memories

Realizing
way too late
she should have moved on

Empty spaces
can only be filled
by those willing to stay
blissfully hanging on the walls
of your life

CALLING HOME

He lets the phone ring
knowing his father is dead
and his mother now must work.

Even the big black dog is gone
though he would not have bothered to answer it anyway

The rattle of the Sea Beach
Coney Island bound subway cars
fill the empty house with the echo
of a thousand screamed at memories

And the boyhood fights of four brothers
come to crystal clarity
as the no voice coming back to him receiver
shakes a little in his hand.

Still - he does not hang up
as a calm comes over him

And a small laugh begins to take shape
in the distant corners of his mind
like a two A.M. dream just before midnight.

Some ancient Rules of the House come forward
like "nights for TV"
It's Joe's night he picks what we watch

Or his favorite
If there is a piece of cake to be divided in two
one brother cuts it – and the other gets his pick
This was the true origin of micro-surgery
Micrometer perfect eight-year-olds
smiling in exact atom splitting perfection

(Really a great rule – This one).

He lets the phone ring
hanging up only
when all memories are exhausted.

Performing his ritual once a week
disappointed - only
when an occasionally visiting brother
happens to pick it up.

**A NOTE ON THE TABLE
WRAPPED IN HER WEDDING RING**

Untied knots
falling like ribbons
from her once young hair

Seeing in her eyes
old promises
betrayed

Children
raised
gone

Wanting more
than the spent shell of a man
she once loved

MY FEARS

My fears bleed inside me
like a young girl's
first menstrual cycle – unexplained
like pioneers
in un-covered wagons
like the first night
in a strange city
like mourners
come to pay respects
like the unsigned goodbye note
in empty house – found
like our sworn protectors
shooting first
like the anxiety of darkness
alone
like the blood red blade
on the chopping block
like my father – mugged
forgetting my name – only
like the finished last meal
of the death row prisoner
like the mad howling
in the murderous night
like drunken drivers
on unlit roads
like the mushroom clouds
of Hiroshima and Nagasaki
like cancer
in inherited genes

I HATE

I hate that "the others" have names

that you are always hungrier
than any man's provisions

that your phone number spells out
We Should See Other People

that you feel the need
to finitely detail ALL your exploits
before – during – and after
each of ours

that I now carry – like a wounded warrior
diseases of other men's fields of glory

that I have become so much less
than the man I was
for the woman you are

that the pulse of my story
beats from a chest not my own

But most of all
I hate that "the others" have names

PTSD AND ME

We stare at each other
just for a minute
as I take the chair opposite his
his desk between us

And he asks – with what seems like
disinterest in his Egyptian accented voice
"How are you doing?"

"Okay," I say
before going into things
(usually not about myself)
that are bothering me
which he writes on the back of some sort
of attendance sheet
nods his head s l o w l y
up and down

And asks me once again
for the date of my birth
so he can electronically send my
seven Clonazepam a day prescription
to my drug store

To keep me calm enough to write
and not to start a fight
at the first perceived slight
that comes my way

FOR C

If I could go back
to the moment
before it was too late
I would not bite my tongue
to your nothing to live for
un-casual comment

I would block that ledge
before you could straddle it
manically grinning

I would hold onto you
as tightly as you did your fears

I would convey to you
in shouted truths
all the loving things
that others did not know
you needed to hear

I would swear to God
or who or whatever you believed in
that You – Do – Matter

I would not have allowed you
to allow me
to be the one with you

If I could go back
to the moment
before it was too late
I would not
have let you go

STRETCH
       (One of Our Roadies)

His 1969 Blue Oldsmobile
molded into the shape
of a God placed boulder
just off the side of the midnight
unlit Goshen, New York road
pre-airbags and un-safety belted
sent him headfirst through the windshield
back in the day when the hospital
would not except a parentally faxed "permission to operate" slip

And so – at fifteen years old
even with a father leaving Brooklyn
at a speed present-day NASCAR drivers would envy
our friend – and instrument setup man
bled to death

And the band – and members of five or six other bands
joined as one to mourn him at his wake
knowing how much he loved music
we gathered together – on the last night
when all but family had left
and – sang him on his way

INDIFFERENCE IS WORSE THAN HATE

"You're a distraction."

That's all she said

All she had to

Almost anything
beats distraction

I mean
what the hell is a distraction?

A petty annoyance

A gnat buzzing your ear

Something seen only from the corner of your eye
there one second – gone the next

Hell
I'd rather be a good old-fashioned pain in the ass

EAST VILLAGE – DECEMBER `69

Mr. Bellem
banging the cold radiator
from two flights above
as if it were the janitor's head

And we
all the tenants
who live on the floors between
wishing it were

For nothing seems to stir him
from his basement apartment
next to boiler
warmth

VICEROY – TWENTY-SEVEN CENT SALE

In the old photographs
my mother is "heavyset"
A kind term
as one would apply to a mother

She dresses in dresses
Even – on every day occasions

It is the way of women
of her generation

She is – brown teeth smiling
Smoker since her teens

Tobacco stains un-erasable

But it is the blackness in her lungs
that will make me weep
her passing

HIGH C's

They say
(at least in one movie version)
that the band played on as the Titanic sank into the ocean

I've played in bands
and had some real bad gigs

The 40th Anniversary Party of a Brooklyn "mobbed-up couple"
where the son's toast was:
"To the best friggin mudder and fadder a guy ever had"
comes to mind – along with some tough barroom fights

But trying to hit a B Flat
while sliding into an icy C Sharp Major 7th ocean
has got to make you wish you'd taken that banking job
your father-in-law had offered you
about three months before your ship had sailed.

POETESS

She thinks in light
and writes in darkness

Exposing her innermost thoughts
like fairytale dreams
of childhood fantasies

No omissions of guilt or pain
No – feel sorry for me – weeping stanzas
No odes to Joy

Beautiful stories unfold
in our reader's minds

Until – as in all fairytales
the breadcrumbs lead to horror
the apple to poisoned sleep
and the boiling cauldron
of the real burning
of the crosses of hatred

...FEAR ITSELF

He carries his stories of war
Like a nurse
blood on white shoes

His words
as visible as his wounds

ON THE HOMEFRONT (1968)

In the sacred darkness
of Brooklyn's drunken bars
I grew into somewhat manhood

Tested often by the testosterone bluster
of liquored up brave men
who thought my musician's long hair
a reason to show their – not even closing time beauty
companion
what they do to young hippie faggots
not realizing we were not all always the
peace – flower power – and turn the other cheek – soft
underbellies
to their crew-cut macho manhood bravado

That some – in fact – rejoiced in watching them
attempting to raise themselves
from the slimy barroom floor
they had pictured us
lying prostrated on – for hours to come

ANOTHER FISH TALE

Out in the woods
Deep
beyond any footpath trod
they found him
bullet hole in his back
projectile removed with hunter's knife

Dead since deer season's opening
the police surmised
figured he'd been done in
accidently or otherwise
by a fellow deer killer
who left him there all winter
after hunter smart carefully
covering his tracks
and hightailing it back
to whatever big city he came from

Probably disposing of his rifle
in the nearby river
and telling folks back home
what a bad year it had been for hunting
and how he'd finally decided
to give it up for good
having lost his taste
for the kill

GROWTH PROCESS

I take back
the thousand curses
sworn you

The diseases
wished you

The accidents
prayed for

The injuries
dreamed of

And
replace them
finally

With the indifference
you deserve

FLAMING JACKS

53

He lights his Jack Daniels on fire
and drinks them down
one
two
    in a row

Like the twin explosions
at Hiroshima
and Nagasaki

We watch them
flame down
    his throat

LET'S DO IT

The last bus left ten minutes ago
and I am standing on a street corner
late at night

There are five guys crossing the street toward me
with very – want my wallet – or my life
looks on their faces

And I smile
Knowing
perhaps like my father before me
I'd rather go this way
than rotting away
in a machine hooked up hospital bed
bag of piss at my side
and some poor underpaid schmuck wiping my ass

BENSONHURST, BROOKLYN

The old Italian men come confused
to her Chinese Restaurant door

Once
just days ago
or so it seems

They sipped espresso
in the avenue cafes
read the Italian papers for news from *home*
and talked in hand movement emphasis
of how "the neighborhood" would never change

INEBRIATED ALLURE

She brings focus
to an otherwise undistinguished night
And I watch her
across the crowded bar
Seeing her
only

She brings beauty
to the drab
low-lit-for-a-reason
pit stop of liquid sanctuary
And I watch her
with burning soul
swimming against the tide

She brings brilliance
contrasted by shadowy beings
And I watch her
blinded by the clarity
of her raised eyebrow
corner mouth smile rejection
of all the filth that approaches her

PRAY FOR US SINNERS

Catholic grammar schools
are filled with a powerful silence

Answers to questions
the only words allowed spoken

The silences' power
growing only in non-responses

Becoming deafening
as eternal seconds tick
in brains refusing to remember
where unknown countries lie on the map
or how dangling participles
are diagramed in sentences

Hail Mary's
fall on deaf ears
as a good Sister of Saint Joseph
draws dangerously closer
to your tightening muscles body
unknowing of where the yardstick attack
is about to take place

Until miraculously
There! – THERE! – just below Spain – Sister
That's where Morocco lies
turns her on her orthopedic habited shoes
to ask the kid three seats to your right
the dangling participle question
that would have been harder to answer
than turning water to wine
or even – raising Lazarus from the dead

"A TOAST"

To

All
    moving   on dirt roads
    following the red sun
    sinking between two hills

Never

        seeing Paris again
        hearing its happy city street sounds
        knowing the pleasures of loved one reunions
        after war block parties
        guzzling more and more Bordeaux
        wondering what became of the dead ones
        crying in their loss
        toasting fond memories

        to long gone warriors
        lying in the poppies
        of their misspent youths.

I'M GLAD SHE REMEMBERS ME SUCH

She remembers the old/young me
The drunk
The walk away from no challenge
but from any woman

The comic
drummer
up all night
in every way

She knows nothing
of the hermit writer

Alone
with paper and pen
Alone
with thoughts
Alone
with regrets
Alone
Alone
Alone

EXTRA FINE

I see the beautiful women
of the Starbucks – Mocha – Venti – Latte
extra cream – extra sugar – extra everything you've got
smiling barista mixed into their cup

And wonder how many extra stair master steps they take
to keep their extra fine asses
in such mucho Grande shape

TRUTH AND CONSEQUENCES

Now
that the mushroom cloud
bursting high into the air
is available to all
even crazed demons

It does not seem
such a good idea

Wondering
through constant threat forever's
what the hell
went so terribly wrong

Well too late my friends
you've made your beds
now evaporate into them

WHAT'S RIGHT WITH THE WORLD

The low resonating notes of the jazz trumpet
come from the back right corner of the stage
at the back right corner of the bar
and convey their slow - stretched melody
through everyone in the joint

The horn man's blowin' cool and smooth
and somewhere - outside
the world is probably spinning on as usual

The gambler's, touts and three card Monte players
are still riding the Joe Shmoes to the finish line

The crazies are carrying on two, three, four way
and more way conversations with themselves

The union leaders are working their members
to a frenzy - preparing them to strike
"Gotta get that larger house - second car - big screen TV
that only three dollars more an hour can get us!"

The bankers are conspiring reconfigured adjustable rate
mortgages
with third year balloon payments
that even your best dreamed raises couldn't cover

And the occupiers of All Streets
are now blockin' their fellow ninety-nine percenters
from getting to work

But in here – in here

The horn man's blowin' cool and smooth
the Southern Comfort's doubles flowin'
and if my luck holds
closing time
is still forever away

COINCIDENCE?

Why do all alien abductions
take place in remote parts of the United States
and include some sort of mind control
and anal penetration

Maybe for the same reason
all never seen before monsters
only attack Tokyo

PAY NO ATTENTION

Tomorrows
we believe
are life's silver linings

Promising to forgive
everything wrong with today and some yesterdays

Sad
then
that even with the failure of each new day
we hold out hope for the next

Paying
with the agreed upon price
of our disappointment

Choosing always to believe
the wizard
is truly behind the curtain

ONE GOOD REASON NOT TO

In the summer
of 1945
men, women and children
slept peacefully in New York

It wasn't until
mid-December
that the strange taste
of burning bodies
wafted into their mouths
on the long journey
from Japan

BACKUP

I lost her
somewhere between St. Marks Place
and midnight
she got off the Jim Hart bandwagon
and climbed aboard another musician
One with more polish
and a 1957 Stratocaster

Some tunes
just play out that way

He was a lead man
and I was just a part of the group

And man that cat had vocals
I mean he blew the house down
like some good looking
male Janis Joplin

Look at me
I mean
even picturing me fifty years younger
your heart would never
skip – a beat

THAT'S HER

That's her
ear infections carried - bouncing through the crying nights
worrying her always good grades
playing with her girl scout friends
growing into liking boys

That's her
our baby girl of Barbie Doll and My Little Ponies
            of first time mommy's makeup trying
            smeared upon her face
gazing for hours into the mirror
sharing stories with her imaginary friend

That's her
in the last picture taken
final shot of a roll of thirty-six
See how the wisps of hair caught by the wind
dance across her pretty face

That's her
eyes wide and smiling watching her father's pride
            watching her as he depresses the small
            button
            capturing her in the absolute square
            of her high school honors blushing
            photograph

That's her
after school activities master
president of her high school
full scholarship to Ivy League University
entire life before her

That's her
last seen wearing
            Nothing
                  as they dredged her body
                  from the icy lake

NOT YOUR PARENTS, YOUR WIFE, OR YOUR KIDS

In front of the Veterans hospital
the old warriors sit
swapping stories
only - with each other

Who else could understand
the things you had to do
the things
done to you

RESURRECTION

She says –
"I hope you die – tonight!"
But it's okay
because I already feel tomorrow creeping up on me

It is a sunny day
bathed in the glow of having moved on – without her

Closing the door
on a pile of regrets

Happy movie music
playing in the background of my new life

There is a swagger in my step
for the first time in three years

"I hope you die – tonight!"
She screams

I smile
watching my shadow climb down
from the crucifix
behind her

HE'LL NEVER BE A POET

He asks me how to write poetry

I tell him to go home
fight with your girlfriend
tell her you don't love her anymore
go sit in a cheap motel room
drink cheaper booze
and write your ass off
in the heartfelt pain of alone

He says
"But what about the girl?"

AIMLESS

My mother
dusted and vacuumed every day

Picking a room or two
from the six
duplexed
three over three

She scrubbed
with harsh abrasive cleansers
all the white porcelain
to gleaming perfection

And polished
all the wood
with the elbow greased attention
of a forester caring for her trees
which had somehow come down
with an insect infested disease

And
at the lied up to height of five foot
she moved the furniture
to get under and behind it

She shook her dust mop out
in the tiny backyard to shake the dust out

Unacceptable today – of course
in our eco-friendly climate

Now we gather our dust
on clinging little cloth fiber pads
to bury in the ground

Because
that's never going to come back to bite us in the ass – is it?

ALL THE WORLDS A...

I wander the hallways
on a Sunday night
in late May

Not believing in spirits or ghosts
but haunted
in the quiet hours of predawn
by words left unspoken

Smelling the sweetness of roses
blooming just outside my window

Remembering every rehearsed phrase
as if it were a scene from a play
watched over – and over – and over
until I knew not only my dialogue
but what your response would be

And then
like some neophyte thespian
I lost my place on the page
went up on my lines

And You
ever the professional
turned to the star
just up stage
who never forgot anything
least of all
how to win the heart
of the fair young maiden

ALL THINGS CONSIDERED

Consider the shifting mist
rolling quietly across the city
Block by block
erasing the breaking dawn
Banishing the hope
of brighter expectations
Expunging pleasure memories
like the phantom cat burglar – never caught

Consider the intangible truth
of an obliterated day
born of the grey mood dampness
or eerie tales spun within self
with you – turning on the border of death
mourning for a life not your own
lived out by the misguided hand
of your bad decisions

Consider the sad discovery
that the world did not owe you a living
or someone to love
or be loved by
that all the rotting planks you ever tread
were your own preconceived illusions
magically appearing
before your each next step

SOMETIMES – YOU CAN'T AVOID IT

"Trouble
That's my middle name,"
he said with a sardonic smile
as he threw a Zippo at the unlit cigarette dangling from his mouth

I drank my bourbon down
paying him no attention beyond the unavoidable sound of
his arrogance

"Trouble,"
he repeated slapping his hand on the bar mere inches from
my fives and singles

I motioned for another shot

"Are you listening!" He inquired inches from my one good ear

"Trouble,"
I said,
"It's your middle name – right."

"You got it" - he said
"Better keep it in mind
That's all I'm gonna say"

"Good" - I said
"I was getting tired hearing about it"

He seemed slower than any trouble I'd ever run into
And proved to be none at all

That's all I'm gonna say

NO COVER UP - NO BRAGGING

He kept his shirt sleeves short
Even in winter
Wearing his tattooed number
Like a badge of courage
Fading on his forearm
From lack of polish
The bravest don't shine their honors
They keep the glow within
Knowing it will come out
Anytime it's needed

LEAST COMMON DENOMINATORS

Teachers
  of no one left behind
  catering to the lowest non-achiever mandates
  whittling away the true intellectual talent
  with the boredom of already known

Students
  stalled like lab rats
  in tired of conquering labyrinths
  staring at empty mirrors
  of nothing to reflect upon

POWERLESS

I met Death
He did not wear a hood
nor was he half in shadow
But he had for me a proposition
Could you kill a baby - he said
Of course not - I replied
But what if I would make it worth your while - he smiled
You couldn't! - I exclaimed
What if from this day forth I would stop
                  all drunk driving
                  all cancer
                  all wars
                  all drug overdoses
                  all death
And with his last word a baby appeared before me
And a gun was in my hand
No more death - save his - He prodded
I looked from the baby's smiling face
to the gun in my hand
I
can't - I barely murmured
Your wife
Your children
All spared - He cooed
I looked to the baby
The retort was greater than I'd expected
Death laughed
I am powerless to do any of those things I promised –
His laughter grew
I fired again
Death
      always wins
                  in
                      the end

DARK PASSAGES

"After All I've Done For You!"
She screams in a voice
that sounds as if she'd suffered on a cross
died
and come back
only
to constantly remind me
of her sacrifice

"After all I've done for you?"
She cries into her hands
closely echoing the sound of the door
closing
on my leaving

"after all I've done for you."
she whispers
into the empty night's loneliness
waiting endless
before her

WHAT'S IN A NAME?

We lived on the same block
played ball together
went to the same high school

One Tuesday afternoon
We got called into Mr. Levine's English class
Staring at each other - wondering what had brought us together
waiting for his first words to drop

"Mr. Hart meet Mr. Sidoti of 3rd period English 101
Mr. Sidoti meet Mr. Hart of 1st period English 101
but I suppose you know each other
since you co-wrote "David and Lisa together," he said, without
a hint of a smile in his voice

"I would also suppose that neither of you know
Theodore Isaac Rubin who actually wrote the story
of David and Lisa in his novel Jordi

And after consulting my TV Guide
I noticed that the movie version played on PBS this past
weekend
And further conclude that neither of you Einstein's knew to
watch to the very end
where they have these things called credits appear on the screen
Now credits – for those of us who don't know
list funny little things
like the actors' names – who composed the music
who the producer was – who the director was
and who wrote the work the movie was based on.

But what I would be willing to bet on
is that you both know what that Big red F
on the top of your paper means

I would have given you a G
but the Board of Education wouldn't allow it
besides –knowing you two
you'd probably tell your parents it stood for Great."

FINE – we said at the same time
already simultaneously formulating our explanation
of the Big red F
Hoping our parents would believe – it meant – Fabulous

**JIMMY BEAM, JOHNNY WALKER, JACK
DANIELS
I WAS ONCE SOUTHERN COMFORTED
BY YOUR FRIENDSHIPS** (7/11/2019)

Depressed

as the letter keys

struck

to write this

I

sit

10,959 days

into my sobriety

with every quivering

same shaking desire

of the first

**"I'M NOT IN RIGHT NOW
  PLEASE LEAVE A MESSAGE AFTER THE BEEP"**

Her voice
five months dead
electronically haunting me
as loud as Marley's chains
dragging across the stone cold floors
of my memory

Tearing my eyes
with the echoed dust of desire
the allergic irritant
of futile need
the passionate tenacity
of solemn desperation

NURSED DRINK

His feelings
hidden behind his perfectly chosen words
like a grade school grammarian
of anal punctuation placement

Worried more with syntax
than meaning
he stays
bachelored to his convictions

Always one drink
under the minimum

Never flying high enough
to get shot down

Never daring enough
for engagement

BROOKLYN FRIDAY KNIGHTS

The longneck Rheingold gauntlet
smashed against the bar
challenge accepted
shiny steel
switchblade
quick and cutting
drops another pretender to the floor

And as in times really not more chivalrous
the very tight
white jean fitted lady
leaves with the victor
she did not ride in with

DIFFERENCES

In pride's fleeting moment
he walks from the podium
applause already dying down
and falling totally silent
before he reaches his seat

The poet realizes
in second's span
he will never feel that same acclaim
as his old musician days
when young girls
rushed the stage before he could leave it
literally squealing for his autograph
to touch his arm or leg or long flowing hair
and invite him
to experience so much more
than words – could ever say

DAWN'S EARLY LIGHT

Poems
are written on harder
more brittle paper
than short stories
or sitcom TV scripts
They
are written in darker rooms
filled with loneliness
despair
and acknowledged shortcomings
They
even when computer generated
leave the deep imprint
of spooled ink
and metallic dug impresses

Poems
are written on softer
more supple paper
than news stories
of racially profiled
    criminal activities
    political shenanigans
    financial indiscretions
    child molestations
or the death of your soldier son's
front page pictured
coffin homecoming
Honor Guard at full attention
State Senator handkerchief to eye
General's proud – strong salute
As if they can replace
his warm loving smile
and tender cheek kiss – goodnight

SATURDAY NIGHT

She sat next to me at the bar
She was young and beautiful
And I looked
And knew better

I could see him coming to her from the second he got up
So too – I guess – could she

"I'm in beds" he said - with a smarmy smile that went
perfectly with the line

I took a gulp of my bourbon to help keep my mouth shut

"What kind do you have?" He was persistent

"The kind you'll never see," she said as if she'd put all the
ice from
her drink and an extra scoop from behind the bar into her
response

He looked at her – Hard
Then at me
As if I was somehow to blame
or had fed her the response she would have used on
anyone with a line that bad

I waved the bartender over
with a two finger signal for a double
If I was going to be seated next to her - for any length of
time
I'd better be fortified against an outbreak of laughter
and the hard stares of the men of one-too-many

I wasn't in the mood for a fight - just yet
And there seemed to be a long line of "rejected men"
forming to my left

A I D S FRAPPE
7/21/82

He went downtown
to buy himself a dose of death
wrapped in a 36C – 25 – 35 woman package

Standing
on the corner
disguised in high heels
and sexy attire

A killer
in black stockinged legs
now serving number 29

SPARE PARTS

95

"We were made for each other."
She declared
seven months
before realizing
that Ray
was made better

I didn't mind much
because by then
Judy
had been put together
by a better manufacturer
as well

LIKE A BEE STING

He has worn out his welcome
along with his options

But unlike generations of predecessors
Firing Squad
Big Axe Chopping Block
Guillotine
Hanging
Gas Chamber
Electric Chair

They are going to humanely stick a little needle in his arm
as he listens to Bach or Rock or Rap

And send him off to meet his maker
as if he were stung by a beautiful insect

How much better they will feel

That
in the end
they had become
the painless dentist tooth pullers
of their great-great grandfather's
impacted wisdom tooth dreams

A NEW YORK MINUTE

The epithetic stares
thrown across the subway cars
and school bus aisles
by city kids
of multicultural hatreds taught

Sear into youngblood souls
who have learned not to flinch
or look away

A generational inheritance of traits
in every shade and color
in politics and religion

A glare
that declares better than
any words spoken
that my pain
is greater than yours

And you
are the cause of it!

"YOU ARE LOOKING FOR 'IRONY' OR 'SARCASM'"

In the ghostly echoes
of childhood voices
taunting the bully on
to beat you more
hit you harder
kick you where it hurts the most
your words form to poems
that diminish all their victories
with the vengeance of your success

And as you stand to read
to shame them in their cowardice
your smile grows
as do those of your audience
who have shared – at least in some degree
the "tag" of
Wise guy
or Bitch
because of the curse
of being able to string
more than five comprehensible words together

AUTONOMOUS

99

She's been told
on numerous occasions
she has a heavenly body

And feels
at times of loving's peak
a user and a used

Looking up
or down
on the changing faces

Never seeing a night
through to dawn

Never a dream
of permanent stay

Wanting shadow sewn
to no one

Relief in left – or leaving
closing of the door

Memories
are for insomniacs

And she sleeps
so solitarily well

A NATURAL

The bartender was old
Hell
even by my standards
He was arthritically slow
and his gnarled fingers
had formed in the perfect shape
of a double shot glass
He had trouble with the mixed – fancy drinks
in the big or odd shaped glasses
But this was a local joint
so there were very few
who came for anything but serious drinking
So it came as a complete shock
to all us regulars
when two guys came in
Smith and Wesson revolvers in hands
demanding everything from the register
and that "secret" cigar box under the bar
And Joe
the old barman
came up with a twelve gauge
and blew them both into the red leather booth
opposite the window
Then with some small amount of pain
showing on his drunk veined old face
pressed the nine-one-one digits
on the old pushbutton phone
splitting the barrel from the stock
and leaving it open on the bar
so he'd be clearly empty handed
when the cops arrived
as if it were something he'd done
every damn day of his life

NO WOODEN NICKELS

"Jiminy Crickets," he said
I suppose being a Pinocchio devotee
in his formative years

And although his nose never grew
it was easy to tell when he was lying
which – of course – is why it didn't pay
for him to borrow money from "Baby John" the bookie
and then fabricate a date on which he'd pay it back

Because – truth be known – Baby John
although no genius among men
had a nose for dates and compound rates
and took a very strong stance
when things like that came and went
with apparent lack of interest

DEFENDANT PROTECTION PROGRAM

My Brooklyn
was a series of chalk out lines
a trail of information givers
paid off
holes left in the population
of "I saw the whole thing" believers in good intentions
until there weren't even whispers of the missing

My Brooklyn
bought silence
at the cheapest price possible
a bullet to the mouth
body dump in the middle of the street
better message imprinted
on the red stained story board commercial
than any of those Madison Avenue Ad Agency
Ivy League boys
could ever conjure up

SORRY EXCUSE

Tell me about your father – he said

I went mute
standing at a bar
foot hoisted upon that familiar rail
I realized there was not enough time
or drink to explain – Father/son love

To tell all he taught me
all he explained
        showed
        prodded
        scolded
        loved me through to manhood

How can one convert memories to words

Oh – I suppose I could begin
with my first real memory
of my three year old hospital stay eye operation
waking – patched eye – half seeing him sleeping in hard wooden
chair beside my bed

And end with his mugged beaten head of non-remembrance
finally giving way to death

But I could not begin to describe the life of love – lived between

SHADES

They saturate our beings in torrential downpours of memory

Like smoke and mirrors occupying the darkness of our
imaginations

An exquisite torture

A formless deception of their nonexistence

Clumsily through the hazy grey fog of overwhelming
sentimentality coming to us

Inhabiting the abandoned nostalgic areas of former selves

They are the locked doors and shuttered windows rattling

That sound we hear on the early morning late night creaky step

The unseen images in the pink dissolving ethereal glow

The whining dogs sleeping uncomfortably through their passage

That familiar scent in a year's empty room

They are the rusted, rotting support beams of our decaying
emotions

The constant reminders - of what we should have done –
while there was still time

PASSING ON THE STREET

Her perfection
is her leaving
Had we struck up a conversation
she might have stayed
and my heart would have been shattered
in the countless pieces of disillusionment

We would have
loved
liked
loved
fought
loved
hated
and eventually
she would have left

Her perfection
crosses the corner of
Notturningback
and
Beentherebefore
heading due east up
Thanks for not hurting me again Boulevard

WRONG!

You came prepared
with a pocketful of accusations
and a steel trap mind
set to entrap me
in some medieval twisted plot scenario
existing in your imagination – only

The girl I was talking with
was one I knew as a child
grew up on the same block
and if truth be known
(not that I'd ever tell you)
she would have preferred you over me
any night of the week

AGORAPHOBIA

The map of my world
is shrinking with my age

No longer
do I venture much past
the coffee shops
or bookstores
of neighborhood
walking distance

The subway ride
to the city
once a daily venture

Now seems a straight climb
up the Himalayas
with only a fog obscured view
waiting as reward
to greet me

JOSEPH MICHAEL – THE FIRST

On the night before my father succumbed
finally
to the beating of drug fueled mugging bastards
I held the deep ridged calloused hand
of his fifty-year hard-working life

And
as on the long walks
of my childhood years
he gave me one last
gentle squeeze

That pulses to this day
like the beauty of his heart
on cold remorseful mornings

SHORT CUT

The fallen night
shelters danger
in its shadowy depths

Familiar landscapes
seen anew

Ominous imagined figures
in every doorway

Until
the unmistakable switch
of the blade's opening

And I am lying
in the pooling puddle of self
running out and down
the cobblestoned street

Poems From The Softer Side, my fourth poetry collection, will
be published in 2022. I hope you enjoy, as much as I did,
what was for me, a chance to show those
I love just how much I feel about them.

WIDOWER

I try to write you a poem every day
as if pressing the keyboard **hard**
were some kind of CPR
and I could pound life back into you

I don't know how much longer I can go on
It's hard to make love to a poem
Even one written in letters of love

It's harder still
to sleep in a half-empty bed
or to start a conversation before realizing
I am sitting alone in the room

But most of all
it's hard
living without you

OLD LOVE

My memories
are a bridge
to our love

A bridge
I've tried to burn
a thousand times

Damn
my asbestos retentiveness

THANK YOU – JUST DOESN'T COVER IT

We never needed
to fall back on "the weather"
for conversation

We never ran out of things to say

There was work
and friends
and the children
and their schools
and their activities

But most of all
there was our love

CAPTURED ON A HAPPY DAY

My maternal grandmother
shines her big Mick face
from ancient rooftop photograph

Her flower dress
as fresh as a new bouquet

The clothespins in her hands
the only clue
that she was stopped mid-work
to pose
for her proud husband's
perceptive eye

IN TUNE

She folds the old tablecloth
as did her mother
and hers before her

Until the wrinkles
of the smooth folds
are as familiar
as the smells
of their shared kitchen

And as loving
as the wordless hums
of their unifying melody

AND NOW I SIT AND GIVE HIM CRAYONS

He's gone from crayons
to fishing pole

And I'll be damned
if I can accept his growth

He dropped that pole
for the challenge of leather and wood

And the baseball diamond
seemed to shrink to his size

The baseball was left behind
for his first set of wheels

And he drives faster
than I ever dared

The car naturally
led to girls

And eventually
to that one woman

That one woman
led to marriage

And then
to a son of their own

And now I sit
and give him crayons

And hope a fishing pole
is the furthest thing from his mind.